Different Ears of Animals

by Grace Hansen

Abdo Kids Jumbo is an Imprint of Abdo Kids
abdobooks.com

abdobooks.com

Published by Abdo Kids, a division of ABDO, P.O. Box 398166, Minneapolis, Minnesota 55439.
Copyright © 2024 by Abdo Consulting Group, Inc. International copyrights reserved in all countries.
No part of this book may be reproduced in any form without written permission from the publisher.
Abdo Kids Jumbo™ is a trademark and logo of Abdo Kids.

Printed in the United States of America, North Mankato, Minnesota.

052023

092023

THIS BOOK CONTAINS
RECYCLED MATERIALS

Photo Credits: Getty Images, Shutterstock

Production Contributors: Teddy Borth, Jennie Forsberg, Grace Hansen
Design Contributors: Candice Keimig, Pakou Moua

Library of Congress Control Number: 2022946801
Publisher's Cataloging-in-Publication Data

Names: Hansen, Grace, author.

Title: Different ears of animals / by Grace Hansen

Description: Minneapolis, Minnesota : Abdo Kids, 2024 | Series: Amazing animal features | Includes online
  resources and index.

Identifiers: ISBN 9781098266257 (lib. bdg.) | ISBN 9781098266950 (ebook) | ISBN 9781098267308
  (Read-to-me ebook)

Subjects: LCSH: Animals--Juvenile literature. | Body composition--Juvenile literature. | Ear--Juvenile
  literature. | Zoology--Juvenile literature.

Classification: DDC 591.1--dc23

Table of Contents

Different Ears of Animals

There are many different ears in the animal kingdom. Ear shape and position helps animals survive!

5

Forward-Facing Ears

Predatory animals tend to have forward-facing ears. Their ears help them focus on their **prey**.

Predators often stalk their prey. If they give chase, their ears help them follow their prey while moving quickly.

Movable Ears

Prey often have movable ears. A deer's body and head can stay still while its ears move in different directions. It listens for danger without drawing attention.

Cupped Ears

Nocturnal animals must find food and avoid danger in the dark. Their ears are often cupped. This helps take in more sound.

Bats are **nocturnal**. Their ears are much larger than their heads. These ears help bats use **echolocation**. They squeak and listen for the echo.

Invisible Ears

Animals that fly or swim have invisible ears. Their ears do not pick up **drag noise** while moving through air or water.

Big Ears

Animals that live in very warm places can have big ears. Blood travels through blood vessels in the ears. Heat is released from the body and into the air. This helps keep the animal cool.

Small Ears

Animals that live in very cold places tend to have smaller ears. The ears are also covered in fur. This helps keep heat from leaving the animal's body.

More Animal Ears!

caracal
forward facing

giraffe
movable

koala
cupped

mouse
cupped

pig
movable

red squirrel
movable; tufted
in winter months

Glossary

drag noise – the sound created by resistance to motion through a fluid.

echolocation – the process by which animals such as bats locate objects by emitting sounds and hearing them echoed.

nocturnal – active at night.

predator – an animal that hunts other animals for food. Preying on other animals is predatory.

prey – an animal that is hunted by other animals for food.

stalk – to track and follow.

Index

Visit **abdokids.com** to access crafts, games, videos, and more!